Garden Art and Architecture

Garden Art
and
Architecture

J. E. GRANT WHITE F.I.L.A.

ILLUSTRATED WITH 112 PAGES OF ORIGINAL PHOTOGRAPHS
BY THE AUTHOR

Abelard-Schuman

LONDON   NEW YORK   TORONTO

By the same author
DESIGNING A GARDEN TODAY

© 1968 by J. E. Grant White

First published in Great Britain 1968
First published in U.S.A. 1969

Standard Book No. 200.71574.7
L.C.C.C. No. 68.10341

Printed in England by Butler & Tanner Ltd,
Frome and London

LONDON
Abelard-Schuman Ltd
8 King St
London W.C.2

NEW YORK
Abelard-Schuman Ltd
6 West 57 St
New York 10019

TORONTO
Abelard-Schuman
Canada Limited
1680 Midland Ave.

Introduction

The aim of this book is to take a broad look at what, for want of a better name, are usually termed "garden structures", including at the same time many of those other architectural features which are complementary to the plants and flowers.

I have presented them in a series of photographs which I have taken in numerous gardens both here and abroad, in the hope that they will show some of the fascinating variety such structures can offer, in purpose and design, and their value in enhancing the attractions of a garden by their practical use and because, in so many cases, they form the very essence of a garden picture.

It can add much to the interest and understanding of the subject if we consider first the main architectural influences which have affected the design of European gardens and, consequently, the features found in them. Garden design has always followed closely on the heels of the architectural trend of the day, since many of the famous landscape gardeners of the past were primarily architects, and only at a later stage in their careers did they become attracted to the art of garden planning.

Although both the Greeks and the Romans are known to have had gardens of a kind, it was the Moors who created the first pleasure gardens in Europe to be laid out on a lavish scale of which we have reasonably accurate knowledge.

These nomadic Arabs possessed a remarkable capacity for absorbing and adapting the culture of other countries, and, after conquering Persia, they made their way across North Africa and in A.D. 711 invaded the Iberian peninsula. They succeeded in conquering most of the southern half of Spain and, once established there, they developed a style of building which was an attractive mixture of oriental and Spanish art, and created a magnificent series of mosques, palaces and gardens.

Their art and architecture reached a height of perfection in Granada, a city which perhaps more than any other epitomises the true spirit of the Moors. Here at the Alhambra and at the Generalife—the king's summer palace—they made some of the first real gardens in Europe. Much of their original form has survived until the present day.

The Moorish pattern of building comprised a large number of interconnected compartments lavishly decorated with ornamented stucco and ceramic tiles. The main rooms gradually led into open or partly open courtyards furnished with fountains and plants, so that it was not always possible to say just where the building ended or the garden began.

Water was always an important feature, being treated formally in the shape of pools, basins and canals which were usually enlivened with fountain jets. The planting was predominantly green, though considerable use was made of flowering plants in pots, the general effect aimed at and undoubtedly achieved being a pleasing sense of peace and serenity. Representational art was almost entirely absent, owing to Mohammedan religious precepts, and no use was made of statuary, in contrast to the garden art of many other countries.

Andalusian Spain and its gardens remained predominantly Moorish in character until nearly the end of the fifteenth century when, in 1492, Granada, the last important stronghold of the Arabs, was taken by Ferdinand and Isabella of Spain.

The Moorish style did not have much impact on design in other European countries until several centuries later, largely owing to the important awakening movement which was then starting in and around Florence, and which we know as the Renaissance. This was a great feeling of resurgence from the long years of depression which followed the fall of the Roman Empire and one of its principal aims was to bring back and give new life to the classical arts of ancient Greece and Rome.

These were the ideas which inspired the architects in the great new building development which now sprang up in Italy, affecting not only public buildings but also the growing number of private villas. The new architecture was projected into the garden and was expressed in the design of terraces, stairways, temples and statuary.

This classical movement in art and architecture soon spread into other countries, in particular to France, Austria and Holland, and it persisted in some form or other as an accepted medium for structural design in gardens right from the sixteenth century until the end of the nineteenth century when its value was questioned by William Robinson and others. Even with today's more functional style of architecture, structures and ornaments of classical type may not look entirely out of place in the modern garden if they are carefully chosen and well positioned.

The new architecture of the Italian Renaissance did not reach England until the beginning of the seventeenth century when Inigo Jones—Surveyor of the King's Works—who had been studying the style of the great Italian architect, Andrea Palladio, decided to adopt it for a number of public buildings in England, notably the Banqueting Hall, built in Whitehall in 1619, to which he gave a classical façade. His work was so admired that classical design soon began to be applied to the many private houses which were being built at this time. Now the first real pleasure gardens began to materialise. From the middle of the seventeenth century their development made exceptionally rapid strides. No expense was spared and they grew in importance as a status symbol.

The prevailing keynote was one of formal symmetry calling for an architectural type of garden in which structures and ornaments played an all-important part. Although scarcely any original examples have survived, the Tudor garden is known to have included most of the garden features which are familiar to us today, such as pavilions, gazebos, balustraded terraces, stairways, formal pools and fountains, as well as statuary and ornaments in great variety. Copies of these are still being reproduced to this very day.

In course of time, these gardens became more and more elaborately furnished, and by the time of William and Mary they had become so overburdened with ornamental features, statues, urns and fantastic topiary that they were beginning to become objects of ridicule. This paved the way for the landscape garden which, by the middle of the eighteenth century, under the influence of Lancelot ("Capability") Brown and others, had begun to sweep away all traces of formality.

The landscape trend, strangely enough, was started by an architect, William Kent, who like Inigo Jones before him had spent some considerable time studying in Italy, where the earlier architecture of the Renaissance had by now assumed a freer and more romantic style. The new villas were being built on sites from which there was a fine panorama of the countryside and preferably where old Roman ruins formed a part of the general picture. The old high boundary walls were now seen as an interruption to the view and the garden projected into the landscape.

Kent brought back these ideas to England and soon put them into effect, and although in the landscape phase which followed a great deal of formal architecture was swept away from gardens, it did not mean the end of garden structures. In fact it popularised the introduction of formal classical temples, of which large numbers are still to be found throughout the country. These were followed later by the inclusion of a variety of buildings in the garden intended simply to give a romantic effect, such as mock castles and chapels, as well as carefully constructed "ruins" so placed that they formed part of a studied garden picture. These have become known as "follies", and although some of them were palpably ridiculous, others created striking pictorial effects or at worst a sense of fun, so often lacking in a garden.

Yet another characteristic feature which made its appearance in gardens during this informal landscape phase was the ha-ha. It was a device much favoured by "Capability" Brown, consisting of a wide sunken ditch walled on one side, which was dug along the perimeter of the garden proper, in order to keep out the cattle from the adjoining parkland. It did away with the necessity of fencing and thus permitted a continuous and seemingly unbroken view of grass from the lawns in front of the house into the park. Since it was not intended to be visible, the retaining wall was usually built as plainly as possible, though a few examples are to be found with decorative stonework, as for example at Duncombe Park, Yorkshire. The name ha-ha seems to have arisen from the element of surprise and deception which was connected with this feature.

During the Victorian age art and architecture went through a very mixed and confused period which was reflected in the garden. By then, a fair degree of formality had begun to return to garden layout and there was yet another revival of the Italian style, this time, however, in a somewhat debased form. Once again gardens became loaded with monumental architecture and ornaments, mostly of a very poor quality, owing to the fact that with the growing industrial development they were mass-produced. Horticultural interest in the open was also at a low ebb and plantings consisted mainly of laurels and aucubas in association with garish carpet bedding.

As had happened so many times before, there were the inevitable reactions, this time from a vociferous group of enthusiasts led by

William Robinson, a writer and keen horticulturalist. In *The Wild Garden* and several other books he roundly condemned the current garden fashions, both the formal and the landscape style, advocating a genuine return to natural gardening.

This coincided with the introduction of new and exciting hardy plants from abroad, and marked the start of a movement towards a form of garden in which, perhaps for the first time, the planting assumed as much or even more importance than any structural design. In consequence, many garden owners became such enthusiasts in this direction that it became fashionable to avoid completely the inclusion of ornaments or decorative structures of any kind.

Such an attitude has to some extent persisted right up to the present day, and this has been aggravated and partly justified by the disappearance of the old-time craftsman, and the consequent difficulty of discovering nowadays anything other than badly made reproductions of garden ornaments. Repeated over and over again in moulds using a cement-based medium, such ornaments have still further prejudiced discriminating people against their inclusion in the garden. Even when craftsmen can still be found, the cost of carrying out individual designs in an attractive medium is often prohibitive, while genuine works of art have become even more expensive and are usually on a scale which is much too large for present-day sites.

Another important factor to be borne in mind is that rapidly changing times and the recent social revolution have seen the replacement of the traditional and classical design of buildings by a more functional approach to architecture and greater freedom from influences of the past.

This has done away with many of the decorative details which formerly gave such variety and interest to garden structures. Admittedly such ornamentation was often grossly overdone and no one would wish to return to fussiness. At the same time, any new artistic development in the garden seems very slow to emerge and for the most part merely tends to reflect the architecture of the house, often far from exciting; or else it takes the form of something so extreme that it comes as an unpleasant shock to the usually conservative-minded gardener.

On this account, it seems very well worth while to preserve the better examples of work of the past in the hope that these may serve as an inspiration to produce something comparably attractive, but in a style that suits present-day requirements and methods of construction.

Design

Whatever style is chosen or developed, it needs to be remembered that garden structures, however attractive they may be in themselves, can never be wholly successful unless they form a carefully considered part of the garden as a whole. They must appear to serve some definite purpose, either practical or artistic, to be in the right position, of the right size, and in a medium which either harmonises or makes a pleasing contrast with the general surroundings. They can play a vital part in the success or otherwise of a garden picture, either as the focal point or emphasising the general design.

A fundamental factor in good design is the promotion of a sense of unity, and first and foremost there must always be a definite connection between house and garden. Sympathetic treatment of the architecture and arrangement of garden structures can do much to achieve this, particularly when they are in close proximity or attached to the house.

The Orangery

One of the earliest specialised garden structures was the orangery. This was not necessarily attached to the house, but it was usually closely connected with it and reflected its architectural style. Although it is now very much a thing of the past, it was a very important development, being the forerunner of the greenhouse, the conservatory and the garden room.

The orange, which was one of the earliest and most popular of exotic plants to be cultivated in England and northern France, was planted in large tubs or square wooden boxes, and these were used in formal manner to emphasise and decorate the terrace and the main axial lines of the garden layout. They spent the summer out of doors, but in the autumn the plants were moved into the orangery, where they remained during the winter and spring until danger from frost was over.

As gardens became more elaborate so did the orangeries, many of which even surpassed in elegance and architectural merit the mansion to which they belonged. Many splendid examples are still standing in excellent preservation such as the one at Hampton Court, and the imposing orangery which Sir Christopher Wren designed for Kensington Palace.

In spite of their architectural magnificence the orangeries of the seventeenth and eighteenth centuries were not particularly well suited to the requirements of the plants they housed. Primitive under-floor heating certainly preserved the plants from serious frost damage, but the only light received was from the windows, which were usually confined to the front of the building.

The benefits of top lighting only began to be realised during the nineteenth century when a pioneer of better cultivation of exotic plants appeared in John Loudon (1783–1843), a landscape gardener and writer of a number of gardening books, who took a great interest in the design of garden buildings, plant houses in particular. He carried out a number of practical experiments in curvilinear glazing and perfected a soft iron glazing bar capable of being bent to any required shape. He demonstrated these improved techniques in the form of a house which he built for himself in Porchester Terrace, Bayswater, London, which at the time of writing is still standing. It incorporated a conservatory with a glass dome which formed an integral part of the architectural design.

An exceptionally fine example of a plant house with a glass dome is to be seen in the grounds of Syon House, Brentford, which came into the possession of the Dukes of Northumberland in Tudor times. Syon House was developed and enriched through the ages by a number of famous architects and designers such as Inigo Jones and Robert Adam, while the grounds were remodelled by the great "Capability" Brown. The great conservatory was built by Charles Fowler in the 1820s and the lofty dome with its sweeping curves is unique in size and kind, and now forms one of the many attractive features of Syon Park, which has been developed recently as a Garden Centre open to the public.

Progress of this kind must have received something of a setback as a consequence of a remarkable episode during the earlier part of the nineteenth century, when plans were made for a glass-domed plant house to be constructed near what is now Palmeira Square, Hove, in Sussex. It was to be known as the Antheum.

In view of the scale of the operation and its dramatic consequences it is rather strange that so few people have any knowledge of it, but it is described in considerable detail by Harold Clun in his *History of Famous South Coast Pleasure Resorts*.

He relates how a well-known local botanist, Henry Phillips, conceived a scheme for the erection of a winter garden built in the shape of an enormous dome, larger in diameter than that of St. Paul's Cathedral. It was to house trees, subtropical plants and a large pond for aquatics, and was intended to serve as a popular rendezvous.

Conservatories

Money was raised from the public who, in return for a subscription, were to receive a season ticket entitling them to the full use of the building. Work was put in hand, but as the giant erection began to take shape, some doubts were expressed about the soundness of design of the structure. It was suggested that the famous engineer Rennie should be consulted, but nothing came of it. As the building neared completion, the scaffolding was removed and work was started on the indoor gardens where some thousands of plants were being assembled.

On the very day before the proposed grand opening and as the gardeners were putting the finishing touches to their work, ominous cracking sounds were heard from above. The workmen ran out from the building and only just managed to get clear seconds before the whole structure crashed to the ground. Here it lay, a mass of wreckage for some years, and the unfortunate botanist who had promoted the tragic affair suffered such a shock that he was struck down with blindness.

One reason, perhaps, why the memory of this ill-fated enterprise may have faded so quickly is because twenty years later it was eclipsed by the resounding success of possibly the most outstanding glass edifice of all time, namely, the Crystal Palace, which was erected in London's Hyde Park to house the Great Exhibition of 1851.

Although, strictly speaking, not a garden structure, it had very strong horticultural connections and was the conception of Joseph Paxton, gardener to the Duke of Devonshire. His Grace had been elected chairman of the exhibition committee, and a problem before them was the avoidance of the destruction of some fully grown trees standing on the site, and it had been decided that the exhibition building would have to be of sufficient height and extent to enclose them. However, they failed to agree upon the nature and style of such a structure. The Duke mentioned these difficulties to Paxton, whom he had singled out previously from the Horticultural Society's staff at their gardens at Chiswick, and had offered him the post of head gardener at Chatsworth, his Derbyshire seat, at the surprisingly early age of twenty-three.

Paxton suggested to him that the building should take the form of a huge glasshouse large enough to enclose the trees in question. The Duke, much impressed, passed on Paxton's proposal and a rough sketch plan to the committee, who then asked for a more detailed drawing. This Paxton quickly produced, but the committee was divided about it and it was shelved. But when a copy of his plan was published by a popular journal, his idea so caught the imagination of the public that the committee was compelled to change its mind.

Paxton's plan was adopted and translated into effect through the collaboration of a leading firm of civil engineers, Messrs. Fox, Henderson & Company. The building which resulted was 1,848 feet in length and 408 feet wide, with a transept roof 108 feet high. The glass alone covered 900,000 superficial feet and weighed about 400 tons.

The exhibition was such a success that it was decided to make it a permanent institution. Obviously it could not remain in Hyde Park, and so a new site was found at the summit of Sydenham Hill, some eight miles south of London, where the building was reconstructed and became known as the New Crystal Palace.

By this time Paxton's irrepressible genius was spreading into other and very varied fields and in consequence the construction of the grounds at the new site was delegated to the author's great-grandfather, Edward Milner, who had enjoyed a long association with Paxton. He was originally an apprentice at Chatsworth, later studying in Paris at the Jardin des Plantes, and by this time was a well-known landscape gardener in his own right.

He laid out the grounds at Sydenham in the current neo-Italian style, with a great show of water cascading down the slopes into large fountain basins. The water terminated eventually in an informal lake, on the banks of which were life-size models of prehistoric animals, placed there not just as an exhibition gimmick but in keeping with the growing interest in science and knowledge which the Prince Consort himself did so much to encourage.

The design of the gardens was later severely criticised by William Robinson and the "back to nature" school. Although they were too formal and ornate to meet with today's approval, as is the case with much Victorian design, they suited the public and undoubtedly gave the very large numbers of visitors to the exhibition a great deal of pleasure and satisfaction.

In the course of time the popularity of the "Palace" gradually declined. It was taken over by the Navy during the First World War, a handicap from which it never really recovered, and was finally burned to the ground in 1936.

The Crystal Palace initiated a big vogue for ornamental glasshouses and by late Victorian times the conservatory was universally popular. More often than not, however, it spoiled the appearance of both house and garden because these structures were seldom planned as an integral part of either house or garden and were too frequently ugly in conception. Ultimately, when the inevitable reaction set in against Victorian taste, the conservatory virtually disappeared and for some time the cultivation of tender plants was carried on in a range of plant houses relegated to the kitchen garden area.

With the coming of the large modern picture window and much improved heating facilities, the old conservatory attached to the house has now been largely replaced by the garden room, a part or an extension of the house in which plants are grown and featured and which leads into the garden. Top lighting has been rendered less necessary on account of the very large windows and also owing to the phenomenal development of the cult of "house plants", many of them natives of dark jungles, which require only a modicum of sunlight for their well being.

The Terrace

Another feature closely connected with the house is the terrace, providing a base from which the garden scene can be viewed and from which the principal walks commence. It has always played an important part in the design of a garden except during a phase of the "landscape" era, when it became fashionable to bring rolling grass and cattle right up to the walls of the house.

For comfort and convenience terraces are usually paved, but a large expanse of unbroken paving can produce a very arid effect. This can be mitigated by the use of plants in pots or tubs, provided that they are of suitable size and design, and are so placed that they do not interfere with the free use of the area for sitting or walking.

Relief can also be effected by an ornamental design worked out in the paving itself, using a mixture of materials such as bricks laid on edge to form a margin to panels of stone flagging; or perhaps inserts of tiles, pebbles or granite setts. A highly cobbled surface must be avoided in places where there is likely to be much traffic since this will be uncomfortable to walk on.

The formation of a terrace usually calls for structural work in reshaping the ground, especially in sloping sites, and this offers opportunities for interesting treatment in respect of the retaining walls which are normally necessary. These can be considerably enhanced in appearance if they are finished off with a suitable coping, while piers and buttresses used at intervals to strengthen the walls can be capped with stone on which pots or urns may be stood to good effect.

Where the ground falls away very sharply from the house, retaining walls may have to be built to a considerable height and will thus present a large facing of brick or stonework. While this can be broken by the planting of climbers and wall shrubs at the foot of the wall, it can also be made more interesting by the construction of a recess for a seat or the building of a wall basin.

In addition, the wall may have to be raised to a suitable height above the level of the ground, so that it lessens any risk of a person falling over. A solid parapet wall built up for this purpose is usually unpleasing and can cut off much of the view of a garden when seen from the house. On this account, a more attractive arrangement will be found in some form of balustrading or in making wide openings in the wall and inserting panels of wrought iron.

Many hillside gardens are arranged to advantage in a series of terraces, and this leads to the question of means of access from one level to another.

For many centuries, stretching even as far back as the early Minoan and Egyptian civilisations, steps have been used to perform this function, not just as a practical solution to the problem but because with skilful design they can considerably enhance the character and beauty of a garden.

Steps & Stairways

In the great Italian gardens which were made following the Renaissance, the villas were mostly sited near the top of a hill and this gave the opportunity for the construction of many magnificent garden stairways, often dividing and continuing down on each side of fountain basins and cascades, perhaps rejoining at the bottom of the hill.

There are all kinds of interesting variations in the design of steps, but it should be remembered that good proportions, the arrangements of flights and landings, and keeping a proper relationship to the surroundings can play just as important a part in their attraction as any architectural style or decoration.

Nowadays, garden steps, in line with modern architecture, tend to be far less ornate than in the past, and it is common practice to form them just with flat slabs of natural or precast stone overhanging similar material or using bricks as risers. This does not mean that they need be lacking in character since interest can be provided in a number of ways, perhaps by judicious placing of pots at the top or bottom of the flight, or by a close association of distinctive planting, for instance, a free use of prostrate junipers, yuccas or heaths. Under certain circumstances there may be opportunity for curving or completely semicircular steps radiating from a circular landing, though there is usually a limit to the number which can be formed in this fashion.

The Patio   Performing much the same function as the terrace is the patio, which is generally a paved area used for sitting, and enclosed by walls or other structures giving shelter and seclusion.

The soaring price of land and growing congestion of building in Britain and elsewhere has tended to reduce many present-day garden sites to a simple rectangular plot so small that the construction of the traditional English lawn is hardly practical, and consequently it is replaced to advantage by paving. The limited space also precludes the use of wide boundary plantations of trees and shrubs, and to secure a sense of privacy so dear to the British, fences, walls, screen walling or trellis may have to be substituted. These factors reduce the garden to the form of a small courtyard such as one finds in many parts of southern Europe and thus offer opportunities for somewhat similar treatment.

As in the case of the terrace, variety can be achieved by a careful selection and arrangement of the paving material, and by taking advantage of the enclosing walls which also offer opportunities for interesting treatment such as the installation of a wall basin, the incorporation of panels of screen walling units or wrought iron, or by the use of wall pots and ornamental plaques.

The small size of such gardens by no means precludes horticultural interest. A variety of climbers and shrubs can be grown on the surrounding walls and fences, and a good show of flowers can be had from narrow borders preferably slightly raised above the paving level and arranged along the foot of the walls.

The patio garden lends itself particularly to the use of containers such as ornamental earthenware pots which can give colour and interest in a great variety of ways. Any visit to the south of France, Spain or Portugal readily shows how much can be done in this manner.

The Entrance

In the days when nearly all mansions had to be fortified, the entrance had of necessity to be an integral part of the building. It was usually grim and forbidding and was often strongly defended by a moat, drawbridge and portcullis. When, however, danger from attack receded and the park and pleasure garden began to materialise the entrance was moved away from the house and often sited at a considerable distance from it. Sometimes, no doubt, this was to impress the visitor with the size of the estate but, equally, in order to present a pleasing picture and views of the parkland. The entrance, therefore, began to be closely associated with the development of the garden and in not a few instances it can legitimately be regarded as a garden structure.

The fortified gate houses were replaced by garden lodges situated on one or both sides of the entrance drive and these were frequently backed by trees and shrubs and furnished with ornamental climbers. Their architecture was usually carried out in a style similar to that of the mansion, but during the "romantic" period of the eighteenth and nineteenth centuries a number of quaintly designed garden lodges sprang up, some with thatched roofs and some in pseudo-Gothic style, designed solely for their picturesque effect.

Avenues of trees were planted on each side of the entrance drive and garden urns and vases surmounted the gate piers, thus tending to link the entrance with the garden just as much as with the house.

Gates

Instead of the old iron-studded entrance doors, gates were installed at the entrance through which one could glimpse the park and gardens beyond, and from very early times wrought iron was a favoured medium for gates as it lent itself to all kinds of ornamental patterns. These were made still more elaborate by the introduction from the Continent of repoussé work, which was raised ornamentation on the metal, effected by means of hammering or beating at the back of the sheet. In Regency times, and later on during the nineteenth century, cast iron was also used for gates as well as for balconies, grilles and railings. It can be moulded easily into complicated patterns and is less susceptible to rust than wrought iron.

Although gates can be hung on iron or wooden posts, in most entrances of importance they are hung on brick or stone piers which in the past were frequently decorated with ornamental carvings, perhaps in the form of a coat of arms. These gate piers were given still further importance by the addition of stone finials in the shape of urns, pineapples, balls, baskets of fruit and flowers, as well as being surmounted, on occasion, by iron lanterns.

Nowadays, entrances tend to be much simpler and far less imposing than in the past; in fact, many people deliberately choose to make the entrance somewhat inconspicuous, even on very important properties, and sometimes restrict it to nothing more than a superior farm gate, for the sake of greater privacy.

Pools & Fountains

Of all the structural features of a garden, those connected with water probably offer more scope for variety, imagination and beauty than any other. Water was a vital part of the earliest recorded gardens, particularly in hot climates where all growth depended on it, and almost without exception they included at least a simple pool or well. In England, few of the early gardens of the monks were without a pool or pond, though its prime purpose was to provide them with a supply of fish.

It was not long, however, before the attractions of the sight and sound of water in motion began to be appreciated, and the fountain was developed. At first it was operated by the force of gravity from a supply of water at a higher level, but later, engineers gave considerable attention to this form of water in the garden and power-operated pumps were soon able to throw jets and a series of sprays to a great height.

In the great classical gardens of the eighteenth century ornamental fountains, basins and formal pools were considered an indispensable garden feature and were planned on a scale of magnificence far exceeding anything constructed during the present age. They were made in the form of long canals, of pools, in oblong, octagonal and circular shapes. Often they were raised in the form of a large basin with central and subsidiary fountain jets and given an elaborately carved stone surround.

In pools of importance, it was customary to feature groups of statuary specially designed to take a part in the water display. Among other remarkable examples of this kind are the groups of statuary seen in the gardens of the Palace of Caserta near Naples, where sculptured groups of men are seen squirting water over a bevy of maidens. Poised above another fountain basin in these gardens are three gigantic dolphins, from whose mouths a great gush of water pours into the pool below.

Water is particularly effective when introduced into a sloping site. A very showy device of the Italian garden was the cascade, whereby a massive flow of water poured down a formal incline or over long flights of steps.

Cascades

Owing to the expense and the smaller scale of gardens, this feature is seldom seen today except in informal guise, as in the rock and water garden, where the intention is to reproduce a mountain stream with water cascading from one pool to another.

The formal pool, though still popular today, has become much simpler both in shape and general design, relying on good proportion for effect. Instead of an elaborate carved stone edging, modern pools are often finished off at ground level with a flat stone coping of self-faced York stone. This has the advantage of giving a full view of the water and its reflections, whereas the older raised edging or coping tended to cut it off. There are quite a number of variations of the old fountain jet to be found today and electric pumps have been much improved. Fountain figures are still popular, but classical styles are giving way to a more modern and less representational type of design.

The biggest development of water in the garden in recent times is seen in swimming baths which have become very much of a status symbol, and their popularity has been further stimulated by the great improvements effected in filtration plant and water heating.

Swimming Pools

A swimming pool does not always fit satisfactorily into the general landscape picture and is probably best treated as a functional feature. The majority of pools, other than those for competition and sport, are now being made in an informal shape, and provided that their curving lines have some meaning and show a sense of design they are more interesting than the earlier types which were usually rectangular.

Perhaps one of the most delightful and at the same time practical aspects of a garden is that it provides a place in which it is possible to relax in a semblance of natural surroundings. In consequence, this calls for very comfortable and well arranged sitting places both in the open and under cover.

Garden Houses

This was realised from the earliest times even in the Medieval gardens in England, when a structure known as a mount or mound became popular. It consisted of an elevated platform built up with soil to form a sitting place and usually turfed. It was sited so as to provide views over the garden and the surrounding country. Later, mounts became more architectural and were constructed in brick and timber, but no examples of this kind have survived.

Covered shelters soon followed and took a great variety of forms. As the pleasure garden developed it became fashionable to entertain in the open and some very elaborate garden houses were built to serve as banqueting pavilions. In the eighteenth century, garden houses usually took the form of classical temples in miniature, some of the most famous being at Stourhead and the exceptionally interesting examples at Duncombe and Rievaulx in Yorkshire. They were tastefully decorated and furnished inside, and even today many are still used for entertaining and for shooting parties.

Gazebos

A rather more specialised form of garden house was the gazebo which, as its name implies, was in the nature of a look-out. It was generally sited at the corner of a boundary wall where there was a good view of the road beneath and of the surrounding countryside. In order to obtain the necessary elevation they usually consisted of two floors, the lower one being used as a garden store and the upper one for sitting. They varied greatly in design, mostly following the prevailing architectural fashion.

Owing to changing times and the high cost of walls and building generally, few if any gazebos are built today, although, fortunately, many fine examples have survived.

Arbours

In addition to garden houses and covered shelters, another popular type of structure in this category is the arbour which, as the name suggests, is a sitting place with a leafy canopy. Such features were well known to the ancient Egyptians, who made them by training vines over poles and used them as summer living rooms.

Sometimes in this country they are formed entirely out of trees and shrubs by training the branches of subjects such as yews, limes or hornbeams. More often, however, they are provided with a basic framework either of wood or of wrought iron. A particularly fine example of the latter is to be seen in the "Birdcage Arbour" at Melbourne Hall, Derbyshire, which was originally constructed in wrought iron early in the eighteenth century by the smith, Robert Bakewell, and which has recently been restored.

Nowadays, arbours are still popular but are usually of simple construction, consisting of timber uprights with cross pieces to form a framework for climbers and roses.

A feature closely allied to the arbour is the pergola, which is of Italian origin. In its simplest form it consists of a series of rough poles arranged to support the growths of lemons, vines or other climbers in such a way as to provide a shady walk and protection from the heat of the sun.

Pergolas

In the course of time the original rustic pergola became suitably groomed and much more architectural in character—to take its place in gardens of importance. The rough poles were replaced by piers built in brick and stone or sometimes by classical columns. These were surmounted by heavy cross-beams of dressed timber which were often topped by a lattice of smaller battens.

Although in the English climate protection from the heat of the sun is seldom a prime necessity, the pergola has acquired considerable popularity in gardens here, very largely because it affords excellent facilities for the growing of the many attractive hardy climbers.

A number of handsome pergolas were designed in the earlier part of the twentieth century by the distinguished architect Sir Edwin Lutyens and were imaginatively planted by Miss Gertrude Jekyll, with whom he collaborated in respect of the landscaping.

To be wholly successful, pergolas need very careful placing. Although they are useful for separating portions of a garden, there is always the temptation to run one down the centre of a garden and so cut in two the main vista. In general, they are much better placed either as an extension of the main terrace walk or following down one or both sides of the garden as viewed from the house.

In the small garden a simple pergola can be formed by pairs of unbarked larch posts, each with a cross-piece, arranged at intervals along a walk. The arches so formed can be connected by tarred ropes or by chains, in order to prolong the run of the more vigorous climbers.

Since a pergola tends to concentrate the eye along the narrow vista which it creates, it is very necessary that it should terminate in something worth while. This could take the form of a seat set in an arbour of the same construction as that of the pergola itself. Alternatively, it could end in an attractive figure or a vase on a pedestal backed by a section of yew hedge.

Follies

In contrast to those structures which have been built specifically to serve some practical purpose in the garden, one can find others, particularly in historic gardens, which when first built had no garden connections, but were later incorporated just for picturesque effect. Often they have been adapted for garden use and turned into garden houses, as, for example, oast houses formerly used for the drying of hops for brewing and pigeon houses primarily constructed for rearing birds for food during the winter months. Others, such as fragments of historic ruins, water wheels and well houses, have been drawn into the garden plan since they happened to be there, or with the idea of producing a feeling of romantic interest.

Such a factor played quite a big part in influencing garden design throughout the eighteenth century and some of the nineteenth, when there were recurrent phases of this nature. Not only were existing features of a romantic type preserved in gardens but it became quite a common practice to devise new ones to be passed off as antiquities.

The resulting "follies", as they became known, assumed a great variety of shapes such as small-scale representations of ruined castles, towers, Gothic chapels, archways covered with ivy, country cottages, grottoes and hermits' caves complete with a live hermit. In addition, it was not unusual for old dead trees to be planted, to give still further romantic effect.

Chinese-style garden structures were not uncommon in gardens in the eighteenth century and became very popular for a time following the publication of books written on Chinese buildings and gardens by Sir William Chambers, which included his *Dissertation on Oriental Gardens* (1773). This eminent British architect, who was officially appointed to the Board of Works, was responsible for the design of the well-known Chinese Pagoda in Kew Gardens.

A further spate of Gothic ruins and follies was seen in the nineteenth century, including pseudo-Indian temples, and rustic structures such as root, moss and heather houses. Ridiculous and tawdry as some of these were bound to be, on balance, gardens were the richer for them as they added interest, surprise and, not infrequently, genuine pictorial beauty to the scene.

In the present age, the counterparts of the old follies are perhaps to be seen in some of the spectacular structures erected in exhibition gardens, such as the central tower built to dominate the grounds of the International Garden Show of 1964, held in Vienna, with a revolving restaurant at the top—now a permanent feature of the Donaupark.

In the private garden, follies—apart from those unconsciously brought about by foolish planning—would seem to be relegated to rather trifling features such as antique street lamps, old cartwheels, miniature windmills, and wheelbarrows filled with plants, not to mention the ubiquitous gnome. One is tempted to add to the list some of the more bizarre modern sculpture.

Garden Ornaments

Garden ornaments, though not necessarily structures, are usually to be found in very close association with many of the more important architectural features found in a garden as, for example, walls, pools and fountains.

In the past they played a very important part in the old traditional formal garden, since they were one of the principal means of giving it interest and variety.

Their employment in gardens today is rather more restricted, partly owing to the different styles of architecture and design generally, and partly because gardening enthusiasts can now find such abundant interest in plants. In fact, there are plenty of notable gardens which are completely devoid of garden ornaments and where satisfying pictures have been created solely through the medium of grass, trees and plants.

On the other hand, there are numbers of gardens in which the judicious selection and placing of an ornament could have made all the difference to its pictorial effect. It is seldom fully appreciated how ornaments of the right kind can strengthen the design of a garden by giving it due emphasis at salient points, and how they can help to impart that very desirable quality of unity by closely relating them to the architectural style of the house or by repetition of a motif which helps to link the various parts of a garden.

One of the most obvious uses for an ornament in a garden picture is to make it the focal point, perhaps as the central feature in a formal garden or as the terminating object in a vista or long perspective. When used and spotlighted in this way, however, it is most essential that something is chosen which is really worth while and of suitable proportions.

Urns, Containers

Some of the most popular ornaments are to be found in containers such as urns, vases and pots which naturally lend themselves to garden decoration because of their use in the cultivation of plants.

The original urn of classical times was a receptacle for the ashes of the dead, but later it was introduced into gardens, largely in order to create a sense of atmosphere. During the romantic period of the eighteenth century the design and placing of urns became an important part of garden arrangement. They were placed on gate piers and walls, in alcoves and niches as well as forming individual features on pedestals, often at the junction or termination of garden walks. They were mostly made of lead, though sometimes of stone.

The real urn had a lid or cap, but as these would tend to be lost, the habit grew of filling the urns with soil and using them as containers for flowers. This no doubt led to the designing and manufacture of urn-shaped vases specifically for the growing of plants not only in lead and stone, but also in various stone compositions and in terra-cotta earthenware.

Closely allied to the urn, and similarly employed for giving a finish to the top of piers and to parts of buildings, are finials. Although often urn-like in shape, they are solid and without a removable cap. They are also seen in a variety of shapes such as balls, pyramids, pineapples, and baskets of fruit and flowers. They are mostly made of natural or precast stone, but examples are to be found in wrought iron. In parts of southern Europe pottery finials are common, sometimes having a copper-lustre finish.

With the coming of less ornate styles of design and the cult of the paved patio garden, simple earthenware pots are being increasingly used in the smaller gardens of today. These are mostly based on the old olive oil jars which abound in the Mediterranean and which, when they were eventually made redundant by the use of metal drums, became popular as plant containers in the garden. They can be kept well planted with flowers with little trouble or expense and in their way can give just as good an effect as borders filled with bedding plants, and at much lower cost both in labour and material.

In addition to round vases and pots, containers can be square or oblong, and are also to be found in the form of pottery troughs, stone sinks, wooden tubs, boxes and caissons, as well as in a variety of shapes in concrete, fibre glass and asbestos.

Sculpture

Unlike the decorative plant containers, statuary has no obvious or logical connection with the garden, but in early Greek and Roman times when sculpture held such an important place in the arts, it was common practice to place statues for ornamental effect in streets and open spaces. Later, when the pleasure garden was developed on the grand scale, this fashion was carried on, particularly in the gardens of Italy and France.

With the influence of the Renaissance, the free use of sculpture then spread to English Tudor gardens in the seventeenth century, from which time it has been associated with gardens in England right up to the present day. Naturally its popularity has varied from time to time, and for many years following the Italian revival in the middle of the nineteenth century, when rather poor reproductions of Italian statuary flooded gardens of the period, sculpture went out of fashion. It is only quite recently that interest in it has been revived, mainly by those looking for a garden feature which in these times of acute labour shortage, requires no maintenance.

However, in gardens nowadays, sculpture is used rather sparingly in comparison with the classical era and, more often than not, consists of one good piece chosen for its artistic merits. Under these circumstances there is a tendency to make the garden just a subsidiary setting to show it off, but the ideal should always be to arrange the layout in such a way that the one is complementary to the other.

From a garden point of view perhaps the chief value of sculpture lies in its association with pools and fountains which offer good opportunities for a figure or group to take part in the play of water. Once pools and fountains became established as important features in a garden, much ingenuity was devoted to original treatment of this sort. For example, figures were frequently modelled which appeared to pour water from a chalice or vase; and cherubs nursing a fish spewing water from its mouth was another favourite subject.

Wall fountains also offer particularly good scope for sculptural effect, since the water is usually introduced through a carved mask. These can take the form of the traditional lion's head, dolphin's, boar's and ram's heads, as well as human heads and torsos.

With regard to the more advanced modern sculpture, although in countries such as Sweden this has achieved some degree of popular approval and appreciation, the general gardening public in England and many other countries is very conservative, and so far as garden ornaments are concerned, still strongly favours things of the past rather than of the future.

Sundials

This is well borne out by the fact that the sundial has remained a popular garden ornament for centuries after it ceased to be of practical use.

There are various kinds of sundial, the more conventional type usually consisting of a circular brass or copper dial engraved with the hours which lies horizontally on a flat stone pillar, the time being indicated by the line of the shadow cast on the dial by the gnomon or pointer. Sometimes the dial or a series of dials are placed vertically around the head of the supporting column. An example of the vertical dial is seen also in the wall sundial, either painted on a wooden frame, or carved on a stone built into the wall.

Yet another type of sundial is to be found in a simple adaptation of the armillary sphere (primarily an astronomical instrument), in which the time is indicated by a shadow cast upon a circular band.

Bird Baths

Among the smaller garden ornaments the bird bath has become particularly popular in English gardens, largely owing to the growing absorption of the British in birds and wild life, and because it is easily fitted into the smallest garden. Unfortunately the design and selection of those available is very poor.

They are best raised off the ground on a stem in order to minimise the attentions of cats, and for the birds' comfort, the depth of water should only be an inch or so.

A suitable position is near the windows of the house from which the varieties and amusing activities of the birds can be watched. They can be sited casually on the main terrace or patio. Alternatively, if they are of sufficient size and importance they can occupy a focal point in the garden, such as in the centre of a circle of paving at the junction of paths.

Lighting

One hitherto much-neglected aspect of ornamental gardening is the use of lighting, but at long last there seems to be a growing appreciation of its value.

In the past gardens were often illuminated for special occasions by means of torches, oil lanterns, wax fairy lights and bonfires, but today, with more modern methods, gardens can be provided with permanent structures designed for this purpose. Unfortunately, so many of these are far from attractive in appearance that the pleasing effect which they produce at night is largely discounted by the way in which they detract from the look of the garden in the daytime.

Traditional structures for providing artificial light in the garden are, of course, wrought iron lanterns which can be mounted on piers, fixed over archways or hung from wrought iron brackets projecting from a wall. These fit in well with most garden schemes and, when suitably designed and placed, can enhance the appearance of a garden even in the daytime.

With the coming of gas and electricity during the Victorian industrial age, cast iron became widely used for the construction of lamps and standards, which were usually designed with an exuberance of classical detail and often in very poor taste.

Now concrete and aluminium are popular materials for lighting columns. Many of the earlier types seen in public places were exceptionally ugly and were rightly criticised by the public. More recently, however, better designs have appeared and some of the smaller types can be used in gardens to good effect.

What are known as bollard lights, for use at low levels alongside a path, are also useful, as well as fluorescent tubes concealed under a low rail for lighting walks and drives, but there seems considerable scope yet for the design of garden lighting units which can form an integral part of the design and at the same time be an attractive ornament.

Another form of lighting for the garden is flood lighting, but in this case the less seen of any apparatus for effecting it the better. In fact, whenever possible, the flood lamps themselves should be completely concealed, whether screened by low planting or sunk below ground level and covered with glass. Sometimes, flood lamps can with advantage be placed overhead, perhaps in the branches of a tree, but wherever they are located the beam should always be directed away from the eye of the spectator.

The lighting at night of swimming and ornamental pools is also well worth while, particularly if there are fountain jets, but lamps should be concealed under the coping or recessed into the sides of the pool, an operation which should always be carried out if possible during the construction of the pool, being much more difficult and costly if it has to be done later.

This applies to almost any kind of electrical effect in the garden. Consideration must be given to this matter at a very early stage in the layout, since cables will have to be laid at a considerable depth to avoid danger of cutting into them. Nothing is more annoying than to have grass and shrubs rudely disrupted by the digging of trenches once the garden has been completed.

Some lighting systems are now available whereby the electric current is transformed off the main supply to about 12 volts. This is a big advantage to the amateur who may wish to carry out the lighting himself since, apart from the saving in current, it does away with the potential danger of handling high-voltage current. Kits with assorted lamps suitable for the garden are now available which the amateur can easily assemble himself, including those for use under water.

Green Structures

Many of the keener horticulturists are quite satisfied with a garden structure created almost entirely out of plants, and it cannot be denied that planting can serve this purpose effectively. For example, hedges can take the place of walls; specimen plants, trees or cut yews will make focal points of interest, while vistas, both formal and informal, can be created solely by means of trees and shrubs in a grass setting.

Even so, it needs to be realised that however fascinating such a garden can be, it is dependent upon living things which are constantly changing in shape and size and, in consequence, they may quickly lose the original form planned for them. In fact, only a few years of neglect can disrupt a layout of this nature and can turn what at the outset was a clearly defined picture into a confused jungle.

On the other hand, structures such as are found in the more architectural garden, provided that they are well built, can last for centuries, and can become enhanced through the passage of time.

It is my hope that many of the examples included in this book will afford evidence of this assertion, and will clearly demonstrate that if structures such as these had never been created, gardens would have been very much the poorer. Similarly, in the case of the modern garden, it is to be hoped that new ones, equally worthy, will continue to be conceived and constructed and enjoyed by many generations to come.

Illustrations

The gardens, various features of which have been illustrated, are listed below in
their order of appearance

PLATES

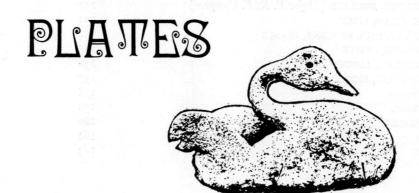

Entrance & Gates

1 SISSINGHURST CASTLE, KENT, ENGLAND. The entrance to this delightful garden is made along a stone-paved path lined with Irish yews and through an old Tudor tower and archway. The grounds were laid out by the late Victoria Sackville-West and her husband the Hon. Sir Harold Nicolson.

2 BRAMHAM PARK, YORKSHIRE, ENGLAND. A part of the forecourt at Bramham Park, the gardens of which are thought to have been laid out in the early eighteenth century by Robert Benson, Lord Bingley.

3 SISSINGHURST CASTLE, KENT, ENGLAND. The east side of the Elizabethan Tower, with brick steps leading down to a rectangular lawn bounded by a yew walk.

4 NYMANS, SUSSEX, ENGLAND. Italian-style archway in boundary wall of the kitchen garden leading out into the extensive woodland which contains numbers of rare rhododendrons, magnolias and eucryphias.

5 HADDON HALL, DERBYSHIRE, ENGLAND. A heavy oak door set in a random-coursed stone wall, which is admirably in keeping with this famous Medieval manor house belonging to the Duke of Rutland. The shrubs on either side are specimens of the yellow-flowered tree paeony, *P. lutea Ludlowii*, a comparatively recent introduction from China.

6 THE ROYAL PAVILION, BRIGHTON, ENGLAND. An imposing entrance to the grounds of this unique residence completed for the Prince Regent in the style of a Hindu palace by John Nash.

7 CASTLE OF PENA, PORTUGAL. Moorish-style entrance to the Pena Palace which stands on a peak in the Sintra hills outside Lisbon, once the site of an old monastery.

8 NEAR CASCAIS, PORTUGAL.   Circular gatehouse and archway at the entrance to a villa on a hill overlooking Cascais.

9 VILLA MAURESQUE, CAP FERRAT, FRANCE. A semicircular stone archway, completely covered by *Ficus repens*, separating the paved forecourt from the garden.

10 ESTORIL, PORTUGAL. In many Continental countries entrances to private houses are closely guarded and screened off. Even so, they can present an attractive appearance, especially when given garden treatment. Here the boundary walls are dressed with formally cut evergreens, and the entrance is surmounted by a pergola carrying ornamental climbers which include bignonias and the large-flowered *Solanum Wenlandii*.

11 "LE PHARE", CAP FERRAT, FRANCE. An attractive entrance to a seaside bungalow, with borders of polyanthus and shrubs in tubs.

12 WONERSH COURT, SURREY, ENGLAND. Attractive treatment of a side entrance to a private house through what was once a stable block. An otherwise blank wall, erected to give the garden privacy, has been relieved by a wrought iron lantern, a bird bath and a pair of spirally trained box plants in tubs.

13 MELBOURNE HALL, DERBYSHIRE, ENGLAND.
A simple but effective gate in cast iron set in
a semicircular archway at the end of the main
terrace. Cast iron had considerable popularity
in the nineteenth century for balconies,
railings, gates and garden ornaments but has
since fallen into disfavour. At the same time,
it has its merits, being more resistant to rust
than wrought iron or mild steel.

14 LOIRE VALLEY, FRANCE. Interesting
treatment in wrought iron of the entrance to
a small villa near Blois, in the valley of the
Loire.

15 VERSAILLES, FRANCE. One of several magnificent entrance gates to the famous palace of Louis XIV whose landscape gardener was the celebrated Le Notre. Although it is uncertain whether he ever actually came to England, there is no doubt that English gardeners went to France to study his style which they later reproduced in gardens in this country.

16 LUTON HOO, BEDFORDSHIRE, ENGLAND. A pair of bronze gates which divide off the terrace from the forecourt. The elegant mansion designed by Robert Adam is famous for its collections of pictures, tapestries and jewellery, and is set off by a beautiful park and garden.

17 ESTORIL, PORTUGAL. Wrought iron entrance gate in front of the tiled porch of a seaside villa.

18 CASA DE NAZARE, ESTORIL, PORTUGAL. The ornamental loggia, helped by well-arranged planting, makes an effective link between house and garden.

19 NEAR CASCAIS, PORTUGAL.   Loggia and balcony of a small modern villa.

20 ESTALAGEM DO CONVENTO, ÓBIDOS PORTUGAL. Elevated loggia with pantiled roof and insertions of glazed coloured tiles in the concrete uprights. In the foreground is a block of roughly dressed stone carrying a lantern to light the garden. The building was once an old convent which has recently been renovated and is now a guest house.

21 HOVE, SUSSEX, ENGLAND. Moorish-style loggia looking on to a lily pool.

22 THE ROYAL PAVILION, BRIGHTON, ENGLAND. A pillared loggia in Hindu style running along the east front of this famous Regency building.

23 IRAKLION, CRETE.   A loggia forming an outdoor room to a small villa in Crete, and flanked by wide concrete arches carrying a framework for climbers.

Terraces & Patios

24 VILLA RUFOLO, RAVELLO, ITALY. The wide floral terrace down below the historic villa built by Nicolo Rufolo in the year 1200, where some six centuries later Richard Wagner was to write *Parsifal*. It is seen here in February bedded out for spring and always maintains a show of bloom throughout the year. The terrace is over 1,000 feet above sea level and overlooks Amalfi and the myriads of vines spread over the hillsides.

25 EVENING HILL, DORSET, ENGLAND. A broad paved terrace with a low parapet wall overlooking Poole Harbour. The stone paving has been relieved and given interest by a design in brick-on-edge, while the surrounding panels have been planted with sods of heather cut from the Dorset moors, in place of turf, thus facilitating maintenance and avoiding the need for constant mowing.

26 ROQUEBRUNE, ALPES MARITIMES, FRANCE. A narrow terrace on the steep hillside overlooking Monte Carlo. Instead of a solid parapet wall, an open effect has been obtained by the use of "screen wall" units, in order to take the fullest advantage of the magnificent prospect over Monaco.

27 ADAMS FARM, SUSSEX, ENGLAND. Simple contemporary treatment given to the extension to an old barn from which a wooden terrace and steps lead down to the garden.

28 TITE STREET, LONDON, ENGLAND. A walled patio garden in Chelsea reached by steps running down from an upper floor of the house, and having an ornamental handrail of wrought iron. The narrow beds round the oval-shaped pool are planted with begonias.

29 TARN HILL, SUSSEX, ENGLAND. Terrace paved with cast stone slabs, interspersed at intervals with exposed aggregate to give more variety. Below the brick retaining wall the treatment becomes less formal with grass and groupings of shrubs.

30 WONERSH COURT, SURREY, ENGLAND. A patio paved with York stone flagging and terminated by a wall fountain on a higher level.

31 EGERTON CRESCENT, LONDON, ENGLAND. A patio garden in Kensington in which the considerable area of stone paving is relieved and made more interesting by a design worked in brick and tiles on edge. The garden is terminated by a wall fountain backed by a high trellis which is smothered in the vigorous growing Russian Vine (*Polygonum baldschuanicum*), making an extremely effective screen and ensuring privacy, even in the heart of London.

32 LA MINOUTIÈRE, FRANCE. Part of an attractive modern garden overlooking the Mediterranean at Beaulieu where the Alpes Maritimes drop very sharply down to the sea, making it a very warm and sheltered region. This necessitates terracing on different levels and skilful handling of steps. Here a stairway from the road entrance descends alongside a high retaining wall to an enclosed patio and is supported by a semicircular archway. Provision for plants has been made by the raised border at the foot of the wall and by pots hung on the wall face.

33 "LE PHARE", CAP FERRAT, FRANCE. Panels of plate glass set in a concrete wall topped by pantiles, which afford protection from the sea winds without cutting off the view.

34 ALLIANCE HOUSE, HOVE, SUSSEX, ENGLAND. Inner courtyard garden of the Alliance Building Society's headquarters with a lawn backed by a long pool, and with flower beds having a paved surround formed of old granite setts.

Cloister Gardens & Walls

35 CHURCH OF ST. JOHN OF THE HERMITS, SICILY.   A pleasant and peaceful garden set in the ruined cloisters of this romantic site. The Arabic Norman church itself dates from the twelfth century.

36 PALACE OF DE CASTRO GUIMARAES, PORTU-GAL. Central cloister garden of the villa, now a public library and museum, which was built by the Count de Castro Guimaraes at the beginning of the present century. It was so planned as to present a pleasing picture from each of the main windows.

37 LA FIORENTINA, CAP FERRAT, FRANCE. Interior of cloister garden contains formal blocks of lavender and other dwarf shrubs standing in a paved surround, while the pillars are clothed with a variety of ornamental climbers.

38 LA FIORENTINA, CAP FERRAT, FRANCE.   Italian-style cloistered garden on the east side of Cap Ferrat affording protection from the sea winds. The carpet of bergenias makes a colourful show of bloom early in the new year.

39 HADDON HALL, DERBYSHIRE, ENGLAND.   Roughly coursed stone retaining wall supporting a grassed terrace and rose garden. Considerable skill is required in building a high wall of this nature. The crevices form a home for rock plants, while at the foot is a border of perennial flowering plants including delphiniums, sidalceas and pinks.

40 SHAFTESBURY, DORSET, ENGLAND.   Wrought iron grille set in an opening in the stone wall surrounding the old abbey. As well as being ornamental it serves a useful purpose, for since it was installed, damage caused by strong winds which sweep over this elevated site onto the plants on the other side has been very much reduced, the opening acting as a release valve.

41 CHÂTEAU DE CARADEUC, BRITTANY, FRANCE. Curving stone stairway leading to the forecourt of this eighteenth-century château situated on a hill with commanding views of the surrounding countryside of Brittany. The forecourt is bounded by chains and stone bollards which originally stood outside the town hall of Rennes and in the centre is a figure of Pan.

42 LUTON HOO, BEDFORDSHIRE, ENGLAND. Random stone retaining wall and stone balustrading to the main terrace at Luton Hoo. Planted in the border at the foot are climbing roses and wall shrubs such as *Cotoneaster horizontalis*.

43 HADDON HALL, DERBYSHIRE, ENGLAND. Upper terrace and balustrading at this famous Medieval home which has been so well preserved. Its history dates back to William the Conqueror and subsequently became bound up with the Vernon and Manners families.

44 VILLA CIMBRONE, RAVELLO, ITALY. Simple but effective balustrading, through which is seen an extensive view of Amalfi and the coast below.

45 HOTEL XENIA, NAUPLION, GREECE. Detail of parapet wall to a broad terrace overlooking the sea and hills. The wall is built of roughly dressed local stone with panels of cast stone, set at intervals, to give contrast and to allow surplus water to run off the paving.

46 PALAZZINA CINESE, SICILY. Ornamental railings surrounding the gardens of an unusual neoclassical villa built in Chinese style, standing in the Parco della Favorita, near Palermo. Running along the top of the railings are a series of bells which pivot and tinkle in the wind.

47 MELBOURNE HALL, DERBYSHIRE, ENGLAND.   Attractively designed wrought iron railings at Melbourne Hall, in the gardens of which wrought ironwork is prominently featured.

48 LE MANOIR DE FERRON, BRITTANY, FRANCE. Interesting treatment of a stairway built in rough stone blocks which leads from the forecourt of the house to gardens on the upper level. The space under the twin flights of steps has been utilised as a garden store entered through a wrought iron gate. Ornamental wrought ironwork has also been used for the stair rail and top landing.

49 HADDON HALL, DERBYSHIRE, ENGLAND. The famous steps by which it is said that Dorothy Vernon slipped away from the ball held to celebrate the marriage of Margaret Vernon to Sir Thomas Stanley, to elope with her lover, John Manners, son of the Earl of Rutland, a courtship of which her family disapproved. The two of them rode through the night to Aylestone, Leicestershire, where they were married.

50 VILLA AT BEAULIEU, FRANCE. What might have been just a long and tedious stairway has been made interesting and attractive by the association of a number of ornamental features such as archways, wrought iron-work and raised flower borders.

51 BRAMHAM PARK, YORKSHIRE, ENGLAND. A curving flight of steps leading from the beautiful house, thought to be by Giacomo Leoni, down to a formal rose garden. The ornamental wrought iron rails to the stairway probably replaced a stone balustrade but are none the less effective.

52 CLAREHAVEN, CAMBRIDGESHIRE, ENGLAND. Shallow semicircular steps leading to the formal rose garden, the focal point being a hexagonal pool. The change of level in what was originally a nearly level site helps to create more interest.

53 MENTON, FRANCE.   Rough stone steps and pergola leading down to a sunken pool, in a garden designed by Humphrey Waterfield.

54 VILLA NOAILLES, FRANCE. Circular steps formed by roughly hewn blocks of local stone on the steep hillside of the Alpes Maritimes. They lead up to a long grass lawn flanked by borders containing a variety of rare shrubs and terminating in a seat formed round a tree.

55 VILLA, CAP FERRAT, FRANCE. Garden steps in reinforced concrete cantilevered out from the side wall. Although they give a modern look, this arrangement presents difficulties in maintenance of the ground beneath, as against a solid flight.

56 ÎLE DE FRANCE, CAP FERRAT, FRANCE. An informally arranged flight of steps with cast stone treads, down a bank planted with shrubs and bold foliage plants such as acanthus and New Zealand flax.

57 ADAMS FARM, SUSSEX, ENGLAND. An informal pool backed by rockwork with grass running right up to the edge. The effect is enhanced by the bank of existing trees at the rear.

58 GENERALIFE PALACE, GRANADA, SPAIN. Patio del Cipres de la Sultana, a courtyard in which the water and fountain jets play a dominating part.

59 MENTON, FRANCE. A long pool terminating in a wall feature with openings of screen-wall units in Humphrey Waterfield's garden at Menton.

60 GARDEN AT HOVE, SUSSEX, ENGLAND. Simple rectangular lily pool with a cast stone paved surround, partially enclosed by a screen wall.

61 CARCAVELOS, PORTUGAL.   A semi-informal pool backed by rockwork and planted with a variety of aquatic rushes and water lilies. The mild climate and nearness to the sea favour the cultivation of bold foliage plants such as bananas and cordylines.

62 NYMANS, SUSSEX, ENGLAND. This Italian fountain is flanked by cut yews which stand at cross paths in the "Wall Garden".

63 ALCAZAR, SEVILLE, SPAIN. Fountain in the spacious marble-floored Patio de las Doncellas, surrounded by graceful columns and intricate plasterwork.

64 DONAUPARK, VIENNA, AUSTRIA. A modern fountain in concrete designed by the celebrated Brazilian landscape architect, Burle Marx. It makes an interesting comparison with that shown in the garden of the Vicomte de Noailles at Grasse (74) which has been carried out in natural stone and with a natural water supply.

65 ALEXANDER PLACE, LONDON, ENGLAND. A wall fountain forming the terminal feature of a small courtyard garden in the heart of London.

66 CHELSEA FLOWER SHOW 1967, ENGLAND. A paved courtyard with a wall fountain and pool designed by J. E. Grant White, F.I.L.A., showing what can be done in an area only 20′ × 20′.

45

67 HOTEL XENIA, NAUPLION, GREECE. A fountain basin and formal pool with a bronze figure in modern style, which form part of the broad terrace to the Xenia Hotel. The paving is formed of smooth pebbles of different colours set in cement.

68 FONDATION MAEGHT, ST. PAUL DE VENCE, FRANCE. A pool by the entrance to the recently completed art centre situated on a hill above Saint Paul.

69 DONAUPARK, VIENNA, AUSTRIA. A very
unusual design for a fountain seen in the
international exhibition held in Vienna in
1964, water being dispensed from tall organ-
like pipes into a large rectangular pool.

70 BRAMHAM PARK, YORKSHIRE, ENGLAND. A grotesque fountain head taking the overflow of water from a large formal basin on the upper level which forms a part of the original layout of the gardens of the Queen Anne house.

71 GENERALIFE PALACE, GRANADA, SPAIN. A part of the water gardens at this famous and beautiful summer palace created by the Sultans of Granada with their innumerable fountains and canals.

2 ST. PAUL DE VENCE, ALPES MARITIMES, FRANCE. Typical Provençal fountain with carved stone head dispensing four jets of water from which the villagers fill their jugs and cans.

3 PIAZZA ARMERINA, SICILY. Old stone fountain—the Fonte Altacura—a central feature of the hilltop gardens overlooking the town. Water comes out of the top of the stone ball and drips down to the basin below.

74 VILLA NOAILLES, FRANCE.   A wall fountain designed by the Vicomte de Noailles in his hillside garden at Grasse. Here a supply of water for the garden is a big problem and it has had to be obtained from a spring in a nearby hill and piped over some distance to this garden.

75 BELTON HOUSE, LINCOLNSHIRE, ENGLAND. A wall fountain flanked by niches each containing an ornamental flower pot, in a part of the gardens of this historic house said to have been built by Sir Christopher Wren in 1685.

76 PALACE OF QUELUX, PORTUGAL. A boldly designed wall fountain standing in the huge forecourt outside the historic royal palace of Quelux. The building, which commenced in 1758, was designed by Matheus Vincente de Oliveira, but the gardens were the work of Jean Robillon.

77 ST. PAUL DE VENCE, ALPES MARITIMES, FRANCE.   Grotesque stone fountain figure and basin standing by the roadside in this interesting little Provençal village noted for its works of art.

78 ATHENS, GREECE. A variation of the wall fountain in marble, forming the central feature of a sitting place which adjoins the Stoa of Attalus, Athens.

Bridges & Cascades

79 STOURHEAD, WILTSHIRE, ENGLAND.   The fine five arch stone bridge which crosses the main garden lake of this magnificent landscape garden. It was largely created by Henry Hoare the younger who anticipated some of the ideas of the professional eighteenth-century landscapists such as "Capability" Brown.

80 STOURHEAD, WILTSHIRE, ENGLAND.   Iron bridge crossing the western arm of the main garden lake, of a later period than the original layout.

81 MOULIN DES RUATS, AVALLON, FRANCE.   A simple but pleasing curved wooden bridge crossing the river into the woodland.

82 PALACE OF CASERTA, NAPLES, ITALY. The Fountain of the Dolphins, perhaps the most impressive of all the series of water features which run the length of the huge park of this royal palace, the building of which was started in 1759.

83 PALACE OF CASERTA, NAPLES, ITALY. The grand cascade designed by Vanvitelli, for which the water supply had to be taken by aqueduct over a distance of twenty-five miles. There is a drop of nearly 250 feet and the water falls into a large basin containing groups of sculpture, including one of Atteone turning into a stag and being attacked by the hounds.

84 PRESTON PARK, BRIGHTON, ENGLAND. Although the formal cascade is very much a thing of the past, rock and water gardens offer good opportunities for informally arranged falls which can give all the appearance of being part of a mountain stream, as can be seen here, where the water is circulated by an electric pump. The thatched shelter fits in well with the general picture. Strange as it may seem it was once a police station.

Swimming Pools

85 SERRE DE LA MADONE, FRANCE.   A swimming pool which still retains a romantic garden atmosphere—seldom easy to accomplish. The pool is fed by a mountain spring and the sides are lined by citrus in earthenware pots.

86 QUINTA DE BACALHOA, PORTUGAL. A large formal basin now used as a swimming pool and part of an old estate, the house of which has been finely restored by Mrs. Orlena Scoville, an American. The interior of the arched pavilion dating from 1450 is faced with Moorish tiles of the 16th century. Princess Margaret was a guest here in 1959 and used to bathe in the pool.

59

87 HOVE, SUSSEX, ENGLAND. An informally shaped swimming pool. The tiled bottom is decorated with a representation of the sun carried out in yellow and black hand-painted tiles.

88 VALE SANTA MARIA, ALBUFEIRA, PORTUGAL. Tiled pool with a shallower section for children. Ornamental seats faced with Portuguese tiles are built out from the surrounding wall.

89 MELBOURNE HALL, DERBYSHIRE, ENGLAND.   An early stone-built garden house. On the side opposite the door is a window overlooking the garden.

90 ADAMS FARM, SUSSEX, ENGLAND.   Part of an old oast house built in Sussex stone which has been converted to serve as a garden house, and forms a dominant feature of the garden, which has been arranged round it.

LA FIORENTINA, CAP FERRAT, FRANCE. An Italianate pavilion on an elevated position overlooking the Mediterranean and the Riviera coast.

92 CHÂTEAU DE VILLANDRY, FRANCE. A garden house in the grounds of the château which was converted in 1532 from an old castle into a fine dwelling by the Secretary of State, Jean le Breton.

93 ÎLE DE FRANCE, CAP FERRAT, FRANCE.   The pavilion in the "Spanish" garden, one of a number of gardens laid out in different styles in the extensive grounds of this old villa.

94 VILLA CIMBRONE, RAVELLO, ITALY. An ornate garden pavilion in Moorish style and incorporating a number of antique Roman, Venetian and Byzantine columns.

95 BRAMHAM PARK, YORKSHIRE, ENGLAND. Stone pavilion with balcony supported by Ionic columns standing at the end of the main terrace walk of this historic mansion, the grounds of which were laid out at the beginning of the eighteenth century.

96 LA FIORENTINA, CAP FERRAT, FRANCE. Interior of Italianate pavilion decorated with ornamental Florentine pots planted with camellias.

97 LUTON HOO, BEDFORDSHIRE, ENGLAND. One of a pair of stone pavilions which are a feature of the large formal garden. They stand on a wide elevated terrace from which are seen views of the surrounding landscape. Part of this garden was originally created by "Capability" Brown, the River Lea being dammed to form an extensive lake.

98 SURREY, ENGLAND. An example of a present-day summerhouse.

99 THE GARDENS, WISLEY, SURREY, ENGLAND. An unusual design for a garden shelter erected in the Royal Horticultural Society's gardens at Wisley to the memory of the Hon. Sir David Bowes Lyon, K.C.V.O., President of the Society from 1953 to 1961.

100 RIEVAULX TERRACE, YORKSHIRE, ENGLAND.   Broad grass terraces occur at Rievaulx similar to those at nearby Duncombe Park and it is thought that they were to be linked eventually into one vast comprehensive scheme. As at Duncombe Park, temples mark key points, the most striking being this Ionic Temple which terminates the long ride, from which an excellent view is obtained of the ruins of Rievaulx Abbey seen down below.

101 STOURHEAD, WILTSHIRE, ENGLAND. The Pantheon Temple designed by the architect, Henry Flitcroft, and suggestive of the Pantheon at Rome. The temple has a fine setting of trees and commands an extensive view over the large informally arranged piece of water typical of the landscape school of design which Henry Hoare the younger anticipated, although he was but an amateur in garden layout.

102 STOURHEAD, WILTSHIRE, ENGLAND. View of the lake from the Sun Temple, seen in the rain.

103 DUNCOMBE PARK, YORKSHIRE, ENGLAND. The Tuscan-style temple which stands on an eminence of the south-west angle of the broad grass terraces at Duncombe Park, the formation of which must have involved a very substantial amount of work, especially using only hand labour. The shaping of the ground is clearly visible around the base of the temple.

104 QUINTA DAS TORRES, PORTUGAL. A charming little stone temple standing in the middle of a formal lake which extends from the walls of the sixteenth-century manor house on the road between Lisbon and Setubal.

105 CHÂTEAU DE CARADEUC, BRITTANY, FRANCE. A stone Temple of Love with a moss-covered dome which stands in a clearing in the woods surrounding the château. The central figure is a statue of Zephyrus the West Wind with butterfly wings and floral crown.

106 ÎLE DE FRANCE, CAP FERRAT, FRANCE. A temple in the grounds of a fine old villa which once belonged to the Barrone Ephrussi de Rothschild and which she presented to the State. The roof of half-round clay pantiles is somewhat unusual for a classical temple but is in keeping with the Mediterranean atmosphere.

107 CHÂTEAU DE MENARS, FRANCE. The Temple of Love designed by Soufflot standing at one end of the magnificent terrace to the château with its fine views on to the Loire. Adjoining the rear of the temple is a large orangery.

73

108 DUNCOMBE PARK, YORKSHIRE, ENGLAND. The Rotunda, one of the remarkable series of temples in the style of Charles Bridgeman built in the early eighteenth century. The Rotunda shown here is thought to have been designed by Sir John Vanbrugh as it is very similar to that which he designed for Stowe.

109 VILLA CIMBRONE, RAVELLO, ITALY. A classical temple with stone columns and a wrought iron dome standing at a high point in the gardens of this celebrated Italian villa, some 1,000 feet above the Gulf of Salerno.

110 CHATSWORTH, DERBYSHIRE, ENGLAND.   The orangery at Chatsworth generally known
as The First Duke's Greenhouse, which contains an interesting collection of camellias
and cool house plants. In front of it is a rose and flower garden dominated by a piece of
sculpture representing Samson and the Philistines.

III CHÂTEAU DE MENARS, FRANCE. Orange
trees put out for the summer from the great
orangery into the conventional white-painted
boxes or caissons which are stood along the
main terrace paths of the château.

II2 CHÂTEAU DE MENARS, FRANCE. This
extensive orangery was designed by Soufflot
and built between 1764 and 1768.

113 SYON PARK, MIDDLESEX, ENGLAND. The Great Plant House built by Charles Fowler *circa* 1820 which is said to have inspired Paxton's design for the Crystal Palace. It is now the focal point of the newly formed Garden Centre in this 200 acre park where examples of every kind of gardening activity are on view to the public.

114 CHATSWORTH, DERBYSHIRE, ENGLAND. Fruit and shrub cases designed and built by Sir Joseph Paxton in 1848 to form what he called the "Conservative Wall". In the central case he planted two specimens of *Camellia reticulata*, a somewhat tender species with exceptionally large flowers and net-veined leaves. These have now reached a considerable size.

115 MENTON, FRANCE.   A somewhat unusual gazebo in the grounds of a Russian-style villa built at the corner of a stone wall and backed by palm and eucalyptus trees. Below are aloes and plants of the sub-tropical *Agave americana*.

Gazebos & Pigeoncotes

116 LEWES, SUSSEX, ENGLAND. A Georgian gazebo in the garden at the rear of an old house in Lewes High Street. The ground falls away to the south very sharply and presents a fine panorama as one looks towards Newhaven.

117 HALES PLACE, KENT, ENGLAND. An early Tudor garden house or gazebo, one of a pair standing at the two corners of the old walled garden.

118 MANOIR D'ANGO, FRANCE. This fabulous pigeoncote stands on a lawn enclosed by a four-sided Renaissance manor, a fine example of the fortified country house, not far from Dieppe. The circular tower is decorated in elaborate patterns of diamonds, squares and chevrons, worked in a variety of building materials.

119 & **120** SERRE DE LA MADONE, FRANCE. A circular pigeoncote standing at the end of an oblong pool adds to the romantic atmosphere of this beautiful garden on a thickly wooded slope of the Alpes Maritimes.

Arbours & Pergolas

121 MELBOURNE HALL, DERBYSHIRE, ENGLAND. The remarkably fine wrought iron arbour known as the "Bird Cage" which forms the terminal feature of the main axis of the garden leading from the house. Plates 122 and 123 show the dome and the view from inside this arbour.

122

123

124 OLD MANOR, SUSSEX, ENGLAND.   An arbour with a stone-paved floor, and stone piers supporting timbers for carrying ornamental climbers, built in the angle formed by an old Sussex barn.

125 CASCAIS, PORTUGAL.   A vine-clad arbour or open gazebo looking out towards the
Atlantic coast.   It incorporates built-in seats and flower boxes planted with petunias.

126 VILLA ROQUEBRUNE, FRANCE. The fascinating garden to this villa had been constructed down a steeply sloping cliff overlooking the Mediterranean. It is full of horticultural interest and the pergola on a levelled terrace hewn out of the rock was built with local stone and rough poles forming a lattice for a variety of ornamental climbers such as wistaria, clematis, *Rosa gigantea* and bougainvilleas.

127 VILLA MAURESQUE, CAP FERRAT, FRANCE. Pergola of classical columns flanking the terrace where Sir Winston Churchill often sat. It is furnished with a variety of ornamental climbers including the evergreen *Clematis Armandii* seen draping the superstructure. An orange tree stands in a bed in the paving.

128 VILLA NOAILLES, FRANCE. An elegant sitting place formed under a semicircular arch supporting an upper terrace, on a sharp slope of the Alpes Maritimes. The shelter is lined with glazed tiles and what appear to be piles of cushions are actually of pottery made in Italy. The floor of the sitting place has a pattern worked in small pebbles.

129 SISSINGHURST CASTLE, KENT, ENGLAND. A decorative wooden seat with distinctive curved back.

130 HÔTEL DE POMPADOUR, FRANCE. A white-painted garden seat in cast iron similar to those used in England in Victorian times.

131 LUTON HOO, BEDFORDSHIRE, ENGLAND. A stone seat facing the formal terrace garden and flanked by herbaceous borders. A yew hedge provides shelter at the rear.

132 GIARDINO PUBLICO, SICILY.   A very quaint structure in the sub-tropical garden at
Taormina which was originally developed by an Englishwoman, Miss Trevelyan, in the
early twentieth century.

Follies

133 BRAMHAM PARK, YORKSHIRE, ENGLAND.   A folly in the form of a miniature chapel in the grounds of this historic Yorkshire garden.

134 BRAMHAM PARK, YORKSHIRE, ENGLAND. Gothic castle-like folly standing on an eminence in the grounds of Bramham Park, and serving as a garden house and look-out.

135 STOURHEAD, WILTSHIRE, ENGLAND. Pretty rustic cottage in Gothic style built expressly as an ornament to the grounds of this early landscape garden and probably used only for tea parties and as a secluded retreat.

Urns & Containers

136 MELBOURNE HALL, DERBYSHIRE, ENGLAND.   This magnificent lead urn on a carved stone plinth stands at the junction of several wide grass walks. It was made by the celebrated Dutch craftsman, Jan van Nost, examples of whose work are found in several English gardens. It was said to be a gift of Queen Anne to Thomas Cooke, her Vice Chamberlain.

37 HEVER CASTLE, KENT, ENGLAND. Lead ⸻nt box filled with pelargoniums at the ⸻de of the steps which lead up to a curving ⸻race walk in this Italian-style garden.

138 LEWES, SUSSEX, ENGLAND. Antique Georgian wine-cooler in grey marble, now used as a container for plants at the rear of an historic house in Lewes High Street.

139 NYMANS, SUSSEX, ENGLAND. A Byzantine-style carved stone urn which forms the central feature of what is known as the Sunk Garden at Nymans, behind which is a stone Italian loggia. The garden was developed by the late Col. Messell and his highly skilled head gardener, James Comber.

140 BELTON HOUSE, LINCOLNSHIRE, ENGLAND. An attractive carved stone container in basket pattern standing on plinth and planted with scented-leaved pelargoniums.

141 PORTIMÃO, ALGARVE, PORTUGAL. Earthenware pots of the oil jar type on the terrace of the Hotel Penina, Portimão.

142 CHÂTEAU DE MENARS, FRANCE. One of the imposing marble urns which are a feature of the main terrace at Menars overlooking the River Loire. The château once belonged to Madame Pompadour, mistress of Louis XIV.

Sculpture

143 CHÂTEAU DE CARADEUC, FRANCE.   A gigantic figure of Louis XIV standing against the curving terminal wall of the main terrace of this Regency period château, one of the finest in Auvergne.

144 SORRENTO, ITALY. A beautiful marble statue in the grounds of an old villa, now an hotel, which was once the site of a Roman amphitheatre.

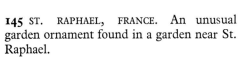

145 ST. RAPHAEL, FRANCE. An unusual garden ornament found in a garden near St. Raphael.

146 CHÂTEAU DE CARADEUC, FRANCE. Carved pillars carrying baskets of fruit and flowers which form part of the building of the Château de Caradeuc, and form a pleasing link with the garden.

147 PALACE OF CASERTA, NAPLES, ITALY. A group of statuary, one of many interesting features associated with the impressive series of cascades, water basins and canals which extend for over a mile through the park of the Royal Palace of Caserta.

148 BELGRAVE SQUARE, LONDON, ENGLAND.   An original model of one of the figures by Jagger which he designed for the Artillery Memorial Group standing at Hyde Park Corner, London. It is the property of Gwen Lady Melchett and forms a feature of the roof garden at her London home.

Sundials and Weathervanes

149 DUNCOMBE PARK, YORKSHIRE, ENGLAND. A figure of Father Time bending over a stone sundial to be seen on the main terrace of this early eighteenth-century landscape garden famous for its series of temples.

150 CHÂTEAU DE MENARS, FRANCE. A large sundial on a circular stone base seen on the terrace of this historic château which stands on the bank of the River Loire.

151 BRAMHAM PARK, YORKSHIRE, ENGLAND. Old stone sundial standing in the centre of the rose garden which occupies the main garden front to this fine house.

101

152 NEWBY HALL, YORKSHIRE, ENGLAND. A combined weathervane and sundial in stone and wrought iron, standing in the forecourt of this famous Adam mansion.

153 VILLA CIMBRONE, RAVELLO, ITALY. An unusual form of sundial seen in the grounds of the villa into which Lord Grimthorpe introduced a great variety of antiquities.

154 FONDATION MAEGHT, ST. PAUL DE VENCE, FRANCE. A striking conception for a weather-vane by J. Miro at this recently established art centre in the Alpes Maritimes.

155 ROYAL GARDENS, ATHENS, GREECE. A marble sundial forming the central feature of a formal garden with ribbon-like beds of violas cut out in the grass lawn.

Lighting

156 ROYAL HOSPITAL, CHELSEA, LONDON, ENGLAND. A lamp supported by an ornamental wrought iron frame which has been used to form the central feature of the gardens of the north-east forecourt to the hospital. It covers the site of an old well.

157 SAN DOMENICO, TAORMINA, SICILY.   A wrought iron lamp standard in the middle of a pool. It forms the central feature of the forecourt to what was once an old monastery.

158 FONTAINEBLEAU, FRANCE.   A cherub bearing a lantern to illuminate a dark corner in a
garden in Fontainebleau, France.

159 CARCAVELOS, PORTUGAL. A modern lamp standard at the entrance to a villa in Portugal. The design reflects that of the old street lamp.

160 FONTAINEBLEAU, FRANCE. A late nineteenth-century lamp standard in cast iron placed so as to light a step in a garden at Fontainebleau, France.

161 A variation of the mushroom type of lighting unit for flower beds in the "night-scaping" range which has the advantage of being a 12 volt system and thereby eliminates the danger of electric shock when handled by amateurs.

162 NAUPLION, GREECE.   A modern mushroom type of unit for lighting flower beds.

163 CASCAIS, PORTUGAL. A simple but effective entrance to a small villa with a wrought iron lantern well placed on a stone pier.